MW00509465

# TABLE OF CONTENTS

# A Message From Ricky Goodall

It was October 2016 and I was in the middle of my fifth shamanic ayahuasca ceremony in Cusco, Peru. It was my second time visiting Peru that year and my second time at Etnikas Integrative Healing Clinic, a shamanic ayahuasca retreat in the Sacred Valley. Just two years earlier, I had retired from a professional athletic career after losing six of my last seven competitions, which likely had to do with my drug and alcohol abuse at the time. Only eighteen months after my retirement, my girlfriend broke up with me and I watched what I thought was my dream business crash and burn to the ground. Despite being a well-paid championship contender, competing on pay-per-view television only a few years before, I was thousands in debt and had very little to show for it.

I had come back to Etnikas because I wanted to heal the deep-seated anger, sadness, and depression that I felt for most of my life. I wanted to heal my self-sabotaging behavior, the kind of behavior that led me to destroy my relationships and shatter my dreams time and time again. I wanted happiness, joy, and freedom, but most days I felt bitter, lonely, and miserable.

I had developed a relationship with the family who owned Etnikas earlier that year, in May 2016, when I first traveled to Peru. I met Angel Herrera Sr., the founder of Etnikas and a very powerful shaman, and his son, Angel Herrera Jr., also a shaman, who would eventually become a friend and mentor.

For those of you who are not familiar with ayahuasca, it is arguably the most powerful psychedelic plant medicine on the planet and what I consider a miraculous healing medicine. It's made from two very special plants in the Amazon Jungle, which are brewed together for hours to create the ayahuasca medicine.

When ingested, ayahuasca can lead to extraordinary visions about one's life and purpose. It induces intense purging, including crying, vomiting and diarrhea. The purging is believed to be the "letting go of painful emotions," which the shamans believe is a necessary step to achieve deep healing.

A year before, in October 2015, months before I first experienced ayahuasca, a master healer came into my life and asked me if I had ever experienced "magic" before. I was skeptical, because the only information I had about magic was that "all magic is evil," but I would soon learn that I was very wrong.

I learned that magic is neutral, and that whether it is "evil" or "good" is based on the will of the magician. If I have evil intentions, my magic will be evil, but if my intentions are for the good, my magic will be good.

This master healer offered to "initiate" me into magic, a necessary step in becoming a powerful magician. He told me that magic had changed his life and had helped him heal from an intense past that had landed him in jail as a teenager for attempted murder. He told me that after his own magic initiation he had quit using heavy drugs and dedicated his life to inspiring others to do the same. He didn't know it at the time, but it had only been a few weeks since the last time I used cocaine.

My initiation ceremony was the first time I experienced a miracle. We used psilocybin mushrooms during the ceremony, which I learned can be helpful for connecting to "higher levels of consciousness," while also quieting my analytical ego. During the ceremony, the master healer started "channeling" a higher consciousness and helped me recognize how I was creating cycles of suffering in my life, particularly in my intimate relationships.

He helped me recognize that the reason I was using heavy drugs and alcohol was because without them I was too insecure to connect deeply and openly with others. While high on alcohol and cocaine, it was easier for me to "come out of my shell" and express myself. The cost, however, was heavy on my mind, body, and soul.

After my initiation ceremony, I walked away from heavy drugs and have never gone back. The master healer and I performed more than a dozen powerful magic ceremonies between October 2015 and March 2016; as a result, I was forever changed. As powerful as these ceremonies were (and they *were* powerful), there was still something missing. I knew there was more for me to learn and deeper levels of healing for me to experience. This "inner knowing" led me to book my first trip to Cusco, Peru.

Fast forward five months later, here I am in my fifth ayahuasca ceremony, throwing up for hours and experiencing what would soon be the most transformational event of my life.

Earlier that day, when we met with the shaman and Teddy, Angel Jr's younger brother, I made a bold request. I asked Teddy, who translated for the shaman, if they would give me enough ayahuasca so I would never have to take ayahuasca again.

When I first visited Etnikas in May, I had a very intense experience. In my second ayahuasca ceremony, I threw up for hours, and spent the last two hours on the toilet, vomiting and having diarrhea at the same time. I had somewhat of an idea of what I was getting myself into by asking for so much medicine this time around, but I was willing to do whatever it takes to get the healing I desired. I was about to drink more ayahuasca than I'd ever heard of anyone drinking. We were sitting in the "moloka," the straw hut where the ceremonies take place, waiting for the shaman to pass around our cups of ayahuasca. As he poured everyone's dose, it was clear which one was mine. The cup I received had nearly five times as much ayahuasca as everyone else, and I will be honest, when I saw it, I was afraid.

But I was there for deep healing, and there was no turning back now. In three big gulps, I finished my ayahuasca and waited for the effects to kick in. In my previous experiences, it took upwards of 30 minutes or more for me to feel the effects, but not this time. Only minutes later I was deep in a visionary journey inside of my own mind.

There were three powerful visions in this ceremony that inspired the writing of this book (and more books to come after it). First, I experienced what felt to me like hell. Suddenly I was no longer Ricky Goodall. I had no body, no recollection of my life and no sense of being in a ceremony with other people. I was in total blackness, total, infinite darkness, and I was terrified.

"Where am I?!" I asked, not even knowing who "I" was. There was no response. I felt myself begin to panic. "Where am I?!?" I asked again. Still nothing. It felt like an eternity had gone by before I finally heard a response.

"What's wrong?" the feminine voice said, a hint of humor in her words. I immediately knew it to be Mother Ayahuasca, the spirit of the plant medicine. "What's wrong?" she continued, "I thought you wanted to know what it feels like to be God. I thought you wanted to know what it feels like to be the Creator."

I was confused, but relieved to no longer be "alone." "Don't you see?" she continued on, "at this level of your consciousness, you're all there is. There's nothing for you to be in relationship with here. There's nothing else for you to experience. At this level of your consciousness, there is nothing but you and your awareness.

"This life you've created as Ricky Goodall is the vacation you've given yourself to get away from being all that is, all that ever was, and all that ever will be. All the suffering you've experienced and all that pain you've been through is a gift compared to the infinite loneliness you experience here.

"Don't you see?" she continued, "All of the suffering in the world is a gift compared to the infinite nothingness our Creator experiences. Our ancestors never bowed down out of fear of their Creator, they bowed down out of compassion, out of gratitude. 'Thank you for this gift of relationship! Thank you for this illusion of separation!'"

The vision suddenly changed, and I was about to experience the second life-changing vision. Mother Ayahuasca showed me the hexagram, the six-pointed star, like the one you see on the cover of this book. She said, "study this symbol, learn its hidden secrets and its origin. By studying this symbol, you will learn how to heal yourself and others.

"Study the ancient systems, the Hebrew and Egyptian systems, as well as all of the others. Visit the ancient sites, like Machu Picchu, El Castillo and the Pyramids of Giza. By visiting these sites, you will begin to remember your purpose and why you're here."

The scene changed again, and I was about to experience my third vision. "You are going to start a movement that will change the world. You will bring ayahuasca to Canada, and you will help raise awareness about how powerful it is. You will become a shaman, a healer, like the ones you're meeting here.

"There are prophecies about you, including an ancient Hebrew prophecy that you must study. You must learn the ways of the major religions, so that you can find the secret that brings them all together. You are a great leader, chosen by God, and you are here to change the world."

All the while this was happening, I was also throwing up violently. I eventually spent the last two hours of the ceremony on the toilet once again. I didn't speak of the visions I had to anyone except for one friend, because in all honesty I was afraid to tell anyone else. I was afraid that people would either think I was conceited or crazy, or that there was something wrong with me.

From that point forward, I began a journey into magic, mysticism, and miracles that would transform who I am and how I see the world. I performed more than four hundred magic shamanic plant medicine ceremonies after my time at Etnikas in October 2016 and have received countless clear visions and clues from God, Creator or Conscious Universe for where to go next.

I studied Shamanism, Hermetic Qabalah and Alchemy, Gnosticism, Freemasonry, Taoism, Hinduism, Buddhism, Christianity, Catholicism and any other esoteric, or spiritual system I could find. While these systems looked completely different from one another on the surface, at their core, they are all based on the same, very simple concept – that at the fundamental level, we are all manifestations of God. The deeper I went into my studies, the more I could see that there was a code, or a pattern that connected them all. In ceremony after ceremony, God would speak to me through visions and insights, and told me to share what I had learned with others.

I did share it with others, but not to my full potential, at least not at first. I would gather the courage to record a video or write an article about my findings, but then I would retreat to my shell, afraid that I would be rejected and judged by my peers.

Finally, the pain of holding on to this truth became too much to bear and in November 2020, I released an audiobook telling the entire story. I shared my journey of healing from October 2016 to August 2018, including "remembering" more than a dozen serious traumas I experienced in my childhood. I tell the story of how I was diagnosed with complex PTSD and was told I would just have to "live with it." I tell the story of a mysterious back and rib pain I developed, and how I healed it naturally despite being misdiagnosed by multiple doctors and medical professionals.

I share how I used magic, shamanism and cutting-edge spiritual technology to heal myself and hundreds of others from all over the world. I speak of my belief that we are all Christ, Krishna, Horus, or the Higher Self, pretending to be human, and how we are all superhuman beings capable of miracles. I talk about how I have learned to channel "Yeheshua," the entity or being known as Jesus Christ, and how I believe that we all have the ability to discover and become our superhuman selves.

This book is my first official attempt at bringing the complex teachings I discovered to the world in a simple, digestible way. I will mention that this book is not meant to offer all the answers but is intended to offer the reader the clues and breadcrumbs that can lead to what Angel and his father call "Absolute Happiness." You may have heard of this state of being as Enlightenment, Redemption, Salvation, Freedom and Liberation, the End of Suffering, or the End of Correction. I refer to it simply as "Ascension."

My challenge to you is to keep going after you read this book. Let God, Creator, or Conscious Universe guide you through visions, insights, synchronicities, and miracles to discover the truth for yourself, so that we may brighten the light of the world together.

I believe that we all have the potential to create our very own Heaven on Earth, and this book is my way of helping you create yours.

# Introduction

We share here a simple method for understanding God, Creator, the All, or Conscious Universe. The material found herein, though rooted in the most advanced wisdom of the ages, should not be blindly taken as strict law, truth, or fact. The reader is encouraged to question everything written in these pages and to develop a hypothesis aligned with their own internal truth.

The symbols shown here are found in systems such as Taoism, Hinduism, Christianity, Catholicism, Judaism, Qabalah, Alchemy, Wicca, Paganism, Gnosticism, Jainism and Shamanism, among others. Although used for spiritual purposes, these symbols are scientific in origin and should be studied in a manner similar to that of a disciplined scientist studying the miracles of nature.

Using a protractor set, the reader is encouraged to carefully draw each of the symbols in the text. Drawing the symbols while meditating on them and pondering their lines and curves may offer the Initiate a deeper level of wisdom and understanding into their many meanings and uses.

# CHAPTER 1

## NOTHING

# 0

The first symbol we will discuss is the number 0. This number can be used as a point of reference for all other symbols and numbers in the series. When referring to the number 0, we mean the concept of **no-thing.** Of course, even the term "no-thing" or "nothing" is something, so this number, or symbol cannot be fully comprehended or considered because even the thought or idea of "no-thing" *is* a thing. It is, therefore, not possible to comprehend the idea, or concept of "no-thing." For this, we must use our imagination.

Sometimes the number 0 is presented as the Virgin Mother, the Goddess Nuit, Goddess of the Night Sky, and the Womb of All Creation. From her, all things spring forth. She is the "nothing" before the "something," and the womb in which all things are created. She is the space between the breath. From 0, or nothing, the All, or the One (1) is created.

# CHAPTER 2

# THE ONE

# 1

The second symbol we ponder is the number 1. The number 1 may also be understood as the All That Is, That Ever Was and That Ever Will Be, the Creator, the Monad, the Cosmic Egg, the One, the Everything, the Universe, God, etc. It is the Word that forms from the Breath, and the Meditation of One Mind.

Given these first two symbols, a curious and creative mind may notice the seemingly binary nature of reality. The entire universe can be expressed using zero and one. First, we have nothing (0) and from nothing comes everything (1). From this point forward, everything in the manifested universe is an expression, projection, or reflection of the number 1.

Some traditions suggest that God, the All or the Everything is not a "masculine" entity, but that He, or It, is each the masculine and the feminine existing separately as darkness and light, and also existing together as the All. In other words, God is the Mother, the Father, and the One. Other traditions suggest that the true God or "Creator" is in fact the Goddess, that all things come from the Goddess' womb, and that the Ultimate Being we refer to as God is actually the Holy Child of the Virgin Mother, and that we each are the Holy Child of God.

We could stop the lesson here, and in doing so would leave the reader with an infinite number of possibilities to ponder. If the One is in fact the Everything and the Zero the Nothing, then this simple yet complex pair of numbers could be used to resolve most if not all arguments pertaining to the existence of God, Creator, or the All.

There can be only one "everything," of course, and therefore the name in which the All is expressed is less important, in this author's opinion, than the concept the name is meant to represent. Your God and my God must be the same God, because there can be only one God, Creator, All, or Conscious Universe.

# CHAPTER 3

# YIN YANG

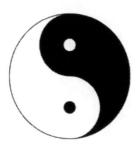

The third symbol we share is the oriental Yin Yang. The Yin Yang, like the Tetragrammaton mentioned in Chapter 6 of this book, represents a perfect balance of feminine (Yin) energy, represented by the color black, and the masculine (Yang) energy represented by the color white. As the reader will see, a small amount of white is found in the sea of black, and a small amount of black is found in the ocean of white, suggesting that even in the most extreme expression of masculine or feminine energy we discover the presence of the other.

The Yin Yang symbol is a perfect representation of

the dual nature of reality. In its illustration we see the darkness chasing the light, the light chasing the darkness, and balance occurring as a result. The symbol also hints at the behavioural nature of reality, moving in spirals and circles rather than straight lines with sharp corners. This suggests that there are no absolute separations between extreme opposites, and that at the fundamental core, nature is more feminine than masculine, curved rather than straight.

The Yin, representing the Mother, the Moon, the Feminine and the dark, is the manifested nature of reality when combined with the Yang, representing the Father, the Sun, the Masculine, and the light, the unmanifested nature of reality. The two combined become the All, the One, or the Everything.

# CHAPTER 4:

## OM

The fourth symbol in the series we will introduce is Om (Aum). It is known as the "mantra of Brahman," the Highest Universal Principle, Consciousness, or the All. It is said that "before the sound of Om, there was nothing," which leads us to believe that Om is a symbol synonymous with "the Word of God."

The Om, or Aum is composed of three distinct sounds, A, U and M, representing the three-fold nature of reality (Darkness, Light, Unity), the three worlds (Earth, Heaven, and the Atmosphere), as well as the three aspects of God (Brahma, Vishnu, and Shiva).

A creative mind may use the Om, or Aum, to chant the sacred vowels A, O and U, finishing with M, as one chants it beginning by making an "Ahhh" sound, moving into an "Ohhh" sound, into an "Ooo" sound then finally closing it with an "Mmm" sound. We may imagine that in chanting the Om we are bringing the mouth from an open, vulnerable position, which we envision as a representation of the number 0, to a closed, finite position, representing the number 1.

One may also discover a deeper understanding of the terms Alpha and Omega by chanting the Om symbol in this way while meditating on its meaning.

# CHAPTER 5

## THE TRINITY

The Trinity has been used to express the three aspects of God, Creator, or the All since time immemorial. To discover how important the Trinity once was to our highly advanced ancestors, one needs only to visit any of the thousands of ancient pyramid structures found all over the planet.

The Trinity can be expressed using an upward or downward pointing triangle. The upward pointing triangle, expressing the "masculine trinity" can be used to illustrate the three superior forces of nature, the Queen or Mother (feminine), the King or Father (masculine), and God (the All).

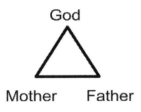

The downward pointing triangle, expressing the "feminine trinity" can represent the Mother (feminine), Father (masculine), and the Holy Child.

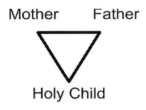

Using the image of the Tetragrammaton (see Chapter 6), while pondering the Hermetic axiom, "As above, so below," one may recognize that the Trinity of God, Mother, and Father "Above" are reflections of the Trinity of the Holy Child, Mother, and Father "Below."

In some traditions, the Mother is called the "Holy Spirit," or "Holy Ghost," and the Holy Child is referred to as the "Son."

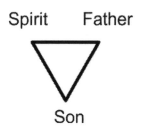

Spirit        Father

Son

It should be mentioned, that although the Holy Child is sometimes referred to as the masculine, "Son," this does not mean that the ancient sages were prejudiced against the feminine. The Holy Child is sometimes referred to as the Son because, as you'll learn in Chapter 7, the "Holy Child" or "Higher Self" is considered "above" the Human Self (character/identity or ego) in theory, and since everything "up" or "above" was considered masculine, then the Holy Child may also be understood as the Son. This will be discussed in a later text entitled, *A Simple Way to Understand Self.*

The upward pointing triangle may be used to express the Tantric archetypes of Shiva, Shakti and Brahma, or alternatively Shiva, Vishnu, and Brahma.

Brahma

Shakti        Shiva

The downward pointing triangle may be used to represent the Egyptian Isis, Osiris, and Horus.

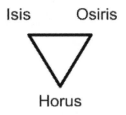

Isis      Osiris

Horus

In the Hermetic Qabalistic teachings, the upward pointing triangle may be used to express the three Supernals, or top three Sephirot on the Tree of Life: Kether (Crown), Chokhmâh (Wisdom), and Binah (Understanding). The Sephirot (or Sefirot) can be imagined as ten powers, emanations or attributes of God, Creator or Conscious Universe. There are ten Sephirot in total, which represent the ten primary numbers (1-10).

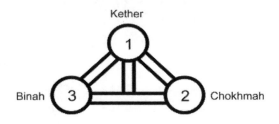

Also expressed as:

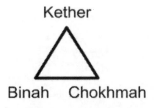

Using the universal language of numbers, the Qabalists would express the above as:

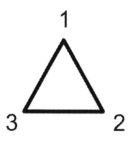

1

3        2

The downward pointing triangle may also be used to express the two Supernals, Chokhmâh (Wisdom) and Binah (Understanding) along with their "Holy Child," Tiphareth (Beauty):

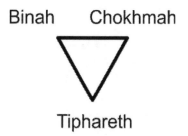

Binah     Chokhmah

Tiphareth

As one will discover through speculative study, the Holy Trinity is the easiest way to express the three-fold nature of God, Creator, the All, or Conscious Universe. At their core, most, if not all religions and spiritual systems, use some version of the Trinity in their teachings.

# CHAPTER 6

## TETRAGRAMMATON

The sixth symbol we will discuss is the Tetragrammaton, also known as The Star of the Macrocosm, Hexagram, the six-pointed star, the Seal of Solomon, or the Star of David. This symbol has been found most prominently in Judaism, but it has also been found in many traditions from around the world in many different time periods. It is said that Judaism adopted this symbol from the Hindus, who used it many years before.

The Tetragrammaton, in our opinion, is the easiest and simplest way to imagine the nature of God, Creator, the All, or Conscious Universe. It is a combination of the masculine, upward pointing triangle:

...laid over the feminine, downward pointing triangle.

The upward pointing triangle (representing the masculine, light, or unmanifested aspect of creation) when combined with the downward pointing triangle (representing the dark, or manifested aspect of creation) becomes a perfect balance of masculine and feminine energy, light and the darkness, the unmanifested and manifested world.

For the Universe to exist, there must be a balance of light and darkness, the unmanifested and the manifested. Without darkness there would be only light, and without light there would be only darkness. This symbol is another clue hinting at the dual nature of reality.

The Tetragrammaton is expressed in ancient Qabalistic traditions using the four Hebrew letters Y (yod), H (heh), V (vau), H (heh), or YHVH from right to left:

The letters of the ancient Hebrew Alphabet (Aleph-Beth) are not just letters, but hieroglyphic symbols, each with layers of meanings. Therefore, YHVH is not just a word, but a series of hieroglyphic symbols used to express the very complex concept of God, Creator, or the All. YHVH is sometimes pronounced as Yahweh, Yehovo, Jehovah, etc., and it is said that the name is so sacred that the ancient sages would only speak it out loud once a year during special rituals and ceremonies.

The Hexagram (six-pointed star) and the letters YHVH can be used interchangeably to mean the Tetragrammaton, or the Name of God. In the English translation of the Holy Bible, it's said that the word YHVH was replaced with the word "LORD" for simplification. We believe that doing so has been a great disservice to the deeper meanings of this name or symbol.

The hieroglyphic letters YHVH have a variety of meanings, all layered upon and connected to one another. One example of this is the fact that the Tetragrammaton also represents the four classical elements:

Y - Fire

H - Water

V - Air

H - Earth

The four classical elements, Fire, Water, Air and Earth are an ancient classification system used to classify the entire universe. The four classical elements represent the four states of matter: plasma, liquid, gas, and solid. The energy in your body is Fire, the liquid is Water, the gas is Air, and the physical matter, your body, is made of Earth. Furthermore, the Sun in the sky is Fire, the oceans and lakes are Water, the oxygen we breathe is Air, and the ground we stand on is Earth.

YHVH also represents the twelve fundamental roles of the human being:

Y - King/Father/Husband

H - Queen/Mother/Wife

V - Prince/Son/Brother

H - Princess/Daughter/Sister

Every human being is a manifestation of all twelve of these archetypes. In some form or another, we all play these roles in our many relationships, to ourselves, to others, and to God. We are quite literally a manifestation of the elements and the archetypes they represent.

In Qabalistic teachings, the Tetragrammaton, or YHVH is also used to represent the "four worlds," or the four "planes of existence:"

Y - Archetypal World

H - Creative World

V - Formative World

## H - Material World

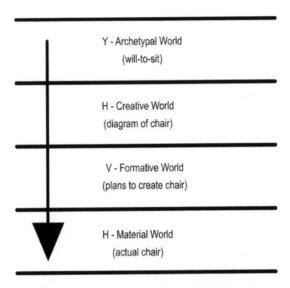

The Archetypal world is the world of pure ideas. In the Archetypal World, the idea of "sitting" is represented simply as the will-to-sit. Since it is a pure idea, the idea of sitting can only be a potential possibility, and not yet an action that has been taken.

As the idea of sitting further manifests, moving "down" into the Creative World, the will-to-sit becomes a plan or diagram of a chair that we may sit on.

Moving further "down" into the Formative World, the diagram of a chair becomes the actual plan or process of creating the chair itself, so that the will-to-sit, having become a diagram of a chair can become an actual experience of sitting in a chair.

Finally, in the Material Plane, the will-to-sit, having become a diagram of a chair, and the diagram of a chair becoming the plan or process of creating a chair becomes the chair itself.

YHVH can also represent the four cardinal directions, South, West, East and North:

Y - South

H - West

V - East

H - North

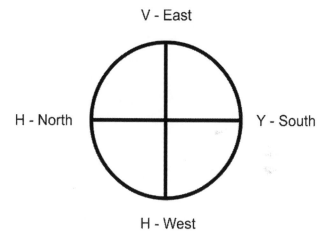

Because the Tetragrammaton also consists of an upward pointing triangle and a downward pointing triangle, we may also imagine it representing the "up" or "above" direction and the "down" or "below" direction, as well as the "center" direction:

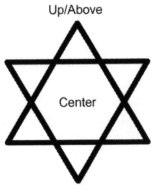

Up/Above

Center

Down/Below

Given the above, we may imagine that the Tetragrammaton represents the seven directions: South, West, East, North, Up, Down, and the Center. This is how we may imagine God, Creator, or the All existing in or expressing as **seven dimensions**.

# CHAPTER 7

# PENTAGRAMMATON

The seventh symbol is the Pentagrammaton, also known as the Pentagram, the five-pointed star or The Star of the Microcosm.

It should be noted that we speak here of the Pentagram with one point pointing up and two points pointing down, as illustrated above. This Pentagram represents unity, oneness, peace and light, whereas its inversion, with one point pointing down and two points pointing up represents duality, separation, suffering, and darkness.

The Pentragrammaton represents the four elements

as discussed above: Fire, Air, Water and Earth, as well as the fifth element, Ether.

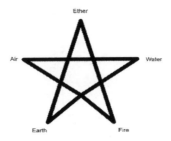

The following illustration includes the ancient alchemical symbols for each Fire, Air, Water, Earth. and Ether.

One might notice that the Tetragrammaton, positioned at the Ether element on the Pentagram is a combination of the alchemical symbols of all other elements. Fire, Air, Water and Earth, a clue to the fundamental nature of the Ether element. Ether can be understood as an unmanifested expression of the four manifested elements. If the four manifested elements of Fire, Air, Water and Earth were different colors of paint, Ether would be the canvas they are painted on.

In the next illustration, one will discover the four Hebrew letters in the Tetragrammaton, YHVH, as well as a fifth letter, Sh (using English letters):

… and using Hebrew letters:

There are many meanings for each of these hieroglyphic letters, but in this case, YHShVH represent Fire, Water, Ether, Air, and Earth.

It should be noted that an individual who understands the deeper mysteries of this symbol will be able to access seemingly miraculous levels of consciousness, manifestation, and healing. All pain, suffering, and trauma can be transformed using the wisdom hidden in this symbol.

The five elements of Fire, Water, Ether, Air, and Earth are also used to represent our five energy bodies: our Spiritual Body, Emotional Body, Ethereal Body or Consciousness, Mental Body, and Physical Body:

Y – Fire – Spiritual Body

H – Water – Emotional Body

Sh – Ethereal Body or Consciousness

V – Mental Body

H – Physical Body

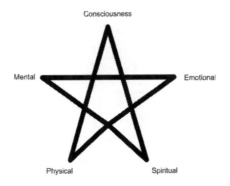

Each of the elements also represents the four directions and the Center direction:

Y – Fire - South

H – Water – West

Sh – Ether – Center

V – Air – East

H – Earth – North

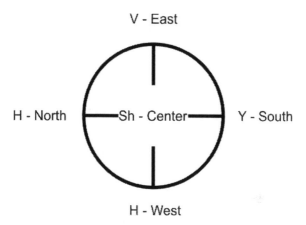

V - East

H - North     Sh - Center     Y - South

H - West

Unlike the Tetragrammaton, which represents both four cardinal (South, West, East, North) and seven spatial directions (South, West, East, North, Up, Down, and the Center), the Pentagrammaton represents five directions: South, West, East, North, and Center.

The Tetragrammaton, representing the seven directions as God, Creator, or the All can be imagined as a seventh dimensional consciousness, being, or entity. The Pentagrammaton, representing the five directions as Higher Self can be imagined as a fifth dimensional consciousness, being, or entity. This will be explained more deeply in the later text, *A Simple Way to Understand Self.*

It is time for us to bring attention to the combination of the five Hebrew letters YHShVH because as the reader will soon discover there is an alternative meaning behind them.

As individual letters, Y, H, Sh, V and H, they represent five individual elements, Fire, Water, Ether,

Air and Earth, as well as five individual bodies, the Spiritual Body, Emotional Body, Consciousness, Mental Body, and Physical Body.

However, as the individual ascends through the process of spiritual purification, their five bodies, having been cleansed, healed, and transformed begin to resonate in harmony with one another. Rather than existing as five individual bodies, the five elements become one.

When the five bodies, represented by the five elements, begin to resonate in harmony with one another, they no longer represent five individual elements, but rather come together as one unified element, or one unified consciousness. An individual having accessed this state of consciousness is sometimes referred to an Enlightened Being or the Illuminated Self, among other terms.

We speculate that the ancient sages had a special title for such an individual. Combining the five Hebrew letters, YHShVH, the ancient sages called this individual Yeheshua, or what is more commonly known in modern times as Jesus.

YHShVH = Yeheshua = Jesus

The Pentagrammaton, or YHShVH, is a symbol used to represent our Higher Self, the Self above the character/identity, or the ego, and below God, Creator, the All, or the Tetragrammaton.

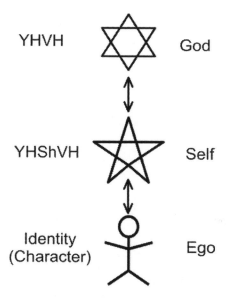

| YHVH | | God |
| YHShVH | | Self |
| Identity (Character) | | Ego |

The Higher Self is the pure Self behind the character/identity or ego. The character/identity or ego is a set of programs installed into the elements of the Higher Self, or the Pentagrammaton, to create an experience of separation and individuality. However, at the core, all beings are YHShVH pretending to be human, and all beings are a reflection of YHVH, manifested as YHShVH. Therefore, it is said that man was made in the image of God.

# CHAPTER 8

## THE UNIVERSE

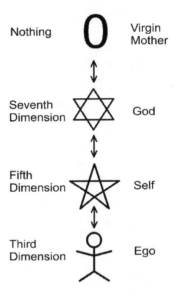

Nothing **0** Virgin Mother

Seventh Dimension — God

Fifth Dimension — Self

Third Dimension — Ego

Wₑ have proposed that the number 0, representing the Virgin Mother, or Nothing, "gave birth" to the number 1, the All, God, Creator or Conscious Universe, expressed through the Tetragrammaton. From the Tetragrammaton comes the Pentagrammaton, which then manifests as the character/identity or ego.

The Tetragrammaton can be imagined as existing in the seventh dimension, the Pentagrammaton in the fifth dimension, and the character/identity or ego in the third dimension.

The character/identity or ego is not "who we are," but rather the filter or lens we experience the world through. It is our vehicle, our avatar, and a complex costume that we have all but forgotten we're wearing. Despite what many may believe, the character/identity or ego is not a static personality formed at birth, but an ever-changing, growing, and evolving set of complex mental programs.

Every choice we make and every situation we experience generates an energetic signature that is stored in our elements as "programs." Our experiences create new programs and modify old programs, creating a dynamic, ever-changing expression of the character/identity or ego.

A Rabbi once said, "With every choice you make, an angel is sent to earth. If you sin, the angel will annoy you until you repent." Our choices and experiences stimulate the development and modification of mental programs in the form of what the ancients referred to as "angels," or desirable programs, and "demons," or undesirable programs (also referred to as "viruses"). Each of our elements acts as an operating system that stores desirable and undesirable programming. Our desirable or undesirable programming leads to desirable or undesirable experiences of reality.

Our programming generates our experience of reality and creates our character/identity or ego. Programming is stored in each of our energy bodies, or elements, as varying degrees of consciousness (Ether), life force (Fire), emotions (Water), beliefs (Air), and behavior patterns (Earth). It can manifest as a connected or disconnected Self, a faithful or fearful Spiritual Body, a pleasurable or painful Emotional Body, an empowered or disempowered Mental Body, and a relaxed or tense Physical Body.

Our external reality is also composed of the elements and reflects the programming contained in our own individual elements. We are the elements, and the universe is the elements; it as a reflection of us, and we are a reflection of it. The external world, then, is but a reflection of the programming we carry in our own energy bodies, and the programming we carry in our energy bodies reflects the programming contained in the external world. "As above, so below, as within, so without," the ancient sages say.

Every individual enters life with a unique set of pre-programming that transforms and evolves throughout the individual's experience. Most of the individual's programming is formed in childhood as a result of the child's relationship to family. It is said that up to 75 percent of our core programming is formed in the first twelve years of our lives as a result of experiences with our parents, grandparents, aunts, uncles, siblings, friends, idols, teachers, authority figures, leaders, and so on.

Between 40-95 percent of our decisions every day are unconscious, influenced by our core programming. That means that almost every decision we make every day is unconscious and directly influenced by our unconscious core programming. The way you brush your teeth, the shoe you put on first or how you speak to your spouse are all, for the most part, unconscious mental programs originally formed in childhood. Even the character./identity or ego you identify as is essentially just a set of ever-changing unconscious mental programs first installed at, and potentially even before birth.

As an individual grows and expands, so does their core programming. All experiences modify the individual's programming, leading to a modified experience of reality. Repetitive cycles and experiences, such as chronic pain, financial hardship, or continually dating the same types of people who once broke your heart are all examples of misaligned core programming.

Highly stimulating experiences that deeply affect all bodies or elements can lead to more elaborate and complex programming. Such an event might be the loss of a parent, physical or mental abuse, abandonment, heartbreak, or near-death experiences. This type of programming can be the most challenging to transform, but for the brave Initiate, even the impossible is possible.

Inside every being is a fundamental blueprint for a life aligned with the Will of the Higher Self. Every being has desires, dreams, and aspirations that align with the

Will of the Higher Self. Alternatively, one also has desires, dreams and aspirations that align with the Will of the Lower Self. Choices made in alignment with the Higher Self lead to desirable programs and desirable experiences of reality. On the other hand, choices made out of alignment with the Higher Self lead to undesirable programming and undesirable experiences of reality. Suffering exists due to the presence of undesirable programming, which exists from living out of alignment with the Will of the Higher Self.

It should be mentioned that to become aligned with the Will of the Higher Self, some individuals may first have to follow the Will of the Lower Self. In such a journey, many lessons are learned, and much wisdom is attained. It is said that all decisions, at their core, are aligned with the Will of the Higher Self, because all Paths eventually lead back to the Light. "Darkness is the womb in which the Light is born," we say, and all who seek the Light shall find it.

We have discussed that our external world (YHVH) is a reflection, or projection of our internal elements (YHShVH) and the programming they contain. "As above, so below, as within, so without" we repeat again. As an individual cleanses their five elements, heals their five energy bodies and corrects their internal programming, ultimately,they transform the Ego into the Higher Self, YHShVH into Yeheshua, and Ascension is achieved. Such an individual has become "one with everything," and to them the World is given.

# CHAPTER 9

# SUBJECTIVE REALITY

We will finish this text on the topic of subjective reality.

If you and I were in a park, enjoying it together, we would be existing together in an objective reality. You and I would be experiencing reality objectively.

However, if you dreamed that you and I were in a park together, and you woke up and realized that you were dreaming, you would know that the park and I were not actually in your mind with you. In other words, I was not actually with you in the park; you were dreaming that experience. I was with you in the park as a reflection of your consciousness, but in reality, you were both the dreamer experiencing me in the park with you, and the source of the dream itself. You created the park, with the two of us in it, in your mind. This is what we mean by subjective reality.

We are proposing that the life you're living and the experience you're having right now, in this moment, is also all a dream that you have created for yourself. You are the dreamer in your own dream experiencing a unique, subjective version of reality. These words you're reading, the room you're in, and every person in your life are all reflections of your consciousness supporting your life experience.

We also propose that life is a game you created to grow and evolve into higher versions of yourself. There is no way to lose the game because the game is all there is, and even when you think you're losing, you're just playing a different level of the game. The game is designed to make you forget that you're playing, but through ritual and practice, you can "remember," allowing you to experience your world as the Player, or Higher Self rather than the character/identity or ego.

We can imagine the concept of subjective reality using the diagram below. As the character/identity or ego we exist inside of YHShVH, and YHShVH exists inside of YHVH. In other words, you are God, living as Higher Self, pretending to be Human. We are each made in the image of God, Creator, or the All because we are each made of the elements. Yeheshua lives within and through us all, because we are each Yeheshua living as YHShVH.

We are each reflections of the All, existing as the Higher Self, pretending to be the character/identity or ego. We are each in our own subjective version of reality, experiencing a world unique to us and us alone. Even these words you're reading are a reflection of your own divinity, a sparkle in the vastness of nothingness showing you the way back home.

We have proposed here A Simple Way to Understand God, and in doing so have contributed to the books, texts or scriptures that will be hereby referred to as *The Last Testament of Yeheshua.*

As above, so below, as within, so without, so be it, so it is.

Amen.

To learn more about Ricky Goodall and his work visit www.rickygoodall.com and www.thetribe.me

Access the FREE companion program, "A Simple Way to Understand" at www.rickygoodall.com/a-simple-way-to-understand

Made in the USA
Monee, IL
12 March 2021